what we do

Support Worker

JAMES NIXON

PHOTOGRAPHY BY BOBBY HUMPHREY

FRANKLIN WATTS
LONDON·SYDNEY

First published in 2012 by Franklin Watts

Franklin Watts
338 Euston Road
London NW1 3BH

Franklin Watts Australia
Level 17/207 Kent Street
Sydney, NSW 2000

Planning and production by
Discovery Books Limited
Editor: James Nixon
Design: sprout.uk.com limited
Commissioned photography: Bobby Humphrey

Dewey number: 362.1'4

ISBN: 978 1 4451 0886 5

Printed in China

Franklin Watts is a division of Hachette
Children's Books, an Hachette UK company.

www.hachette.co.uk

The author, packager and publisher would like
to thank Norfolk County Council and
Sprowston Day Services, Norwich, for their
help and participation in this book.

what we do

CONTENTS

Words in **bold** appear in the glossary on page 24.

I AM A SUPPORT WORKER

My name is Dan. I work as a support worker for adults with **learning disabilities** who need help during the day. I am part of a team of 20 staff providing a service for around 100 people. I support people in many different places, sometimes at home or college, in the community or at a day centre.

Some support workers work with other groups of people, such as children or the elderly. The help we provide makes it possible for people to lead **independent** and active lives.

▼ *The day centre is a place where people can meet with friends and plan activities.*

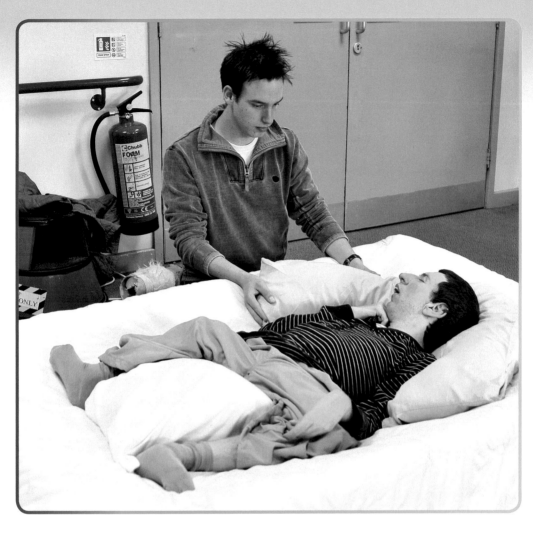

The people I support have a wide range of needs. Some have **physical disabilities** as well as learning disabilities. My job is to assist people in all areas of their lives so that they can do the things they want to do. This might be helping someone to get washed and dressed, to learn new skills or to take part in activities.

I love my job because I am making a difference to people's lives. I would not want to work anywhere else. I enjoy working as part of a team

▲ I always make sure that the people I support are comfortable.

with the other support workers. The most challenging part of my job is supporting people who are anxious or upset.

KEY SKILLS

FRIENDLY AND CARING –
You need the ability to put people at ease, whatever their needs.

BUILDING RELATIONSHIPS

Being a support worker is about offering more than just practical help. We must build good relationships with all of the people we support.

By getting to know a person well, we find out more about their particular interests and practical needs. As we spend more time with a person we try to learn what is important to them and gain their trust. I always make time to chat with people. They might tell me about their activities or how they are feeling.

◄ *People communicate in different ways. This man is expressing himself to show me that he is happy.*

KEY SKILLS

GOOD COMMUNICATION – Support workers must be able to relate with all kinds of people and find different ways to communicate.

Support workers must be good listeners. People often have problems or concerns that we can help with. Some people with learning disabilities have difficulties with communication so we have to find ways to help them express themselves. We look out for signs to show us how someone is feeling, such as being quiet or tearful. The more we work with people, the better we become at understanding them.

▲ Here is Matt, another member of staff. He supports a woman who is upset.

▼ *Some people use a basic form of sign language to communicate. We also have picture cards so people can show us what they want.*

PLANNING SUPPORT

Support workers help people to develop a support plan. This describes how the person wants to be supported and what particular things they need help with.

When someone comes to our services for the first time, a support worker may help to find out what needs to go in their support plan. We talk to the person about what they want their support plan to say.

Writing a support plan is a team effort. We often hold a meeting with the person and their family to discuss their needs and wishes. If we involve everyone who knows the person well, we can help them make better decisions and plans.

▼ *A meeting with a person and their family, friends and support workers is called a 'circle of support'.*

▲ *I talk to a man to make sure he understands his support plan.*

The support plan covers the person's needs, such as help with eating and drinking as well as their wishes for the future. It also describes how to help the person stay independent and make his or her own decisions. A support plan includes **risk assessments** to make sure the person stays safe while taking part in activities.

Any support worker who works with a person must read their support plan first. As you learn more about a person you may see that the plan needs altering.

KEY SKILLS

PROBLEM SOLVING –
As well as working to a plan,
support workers have to react
to situations and solve problems
as they arise.

WORKING WITH OTHERS

Support workers have to work closely with other professionals and the families of the people they support.

If you support a person in their own home you might have lots of contact with their relatives. I keep families up to date with the work I am doing, answer any questions and give them a chance to talk through problems. I sometimes help other professionals, such as **social workers** or **speech therapists**, to assess people's support needs.

▼ *There are often lots of staff involved in a person's life, so we work together to **coordinate** the support we offer.*

**RESPECT AND
SENSITIVITY –**
You must respect the
people you support
and be **sensitive** to their
feelings in everything
you do. You need to
respect their privacy
too. Information about
people must be kept
confidential.

I make sure all relevant
people are kept informed
about what I have been
supporting the person to
do. I report any changes
in the person's needs to
my manager.

If a person has an accident
or some other problem,
I ring their home to let
them know what has
happened. If it is a medical
emergency I might have
to ring an ambulance.

▶ *During an emergency phone
call I have to stay calm and pass
on important information.*

PERSONAL CARE

Personal care means helping people to wash, dress, eat and drink. It is a large part of a support worker's job, especially if you are working with people who have physical disabilities.

You cannot be squeamish as a support worker. Some people need assistance when they go to the toilet. Many need help with bathing and showering. Support workers must be sensitive to people's needs, respect their privacy and make sure they are clean and comfortable.

Support workers assist people as they eat and drink. Some people have problems swallowing and can be vulnerable to choking if food or liquid goes down the wrong way. We help people to choose foods that are suitable for them and check that they do not eat too quickly.

◀ *It is important to help people do as much as possible for themselves.*

KEY SKILLS

KNOWLEDGE OF HEALTH AND HYGIENE – You should have a high standard of cleanliness and understand the importance of health and hygiene.

▲ *My colleague Jodie assists a man as he eats his lunch.*

Everyday tasks like getting dressed can be difficult for people with physical disabilities so we give them support. Some people have specialist clothing which is easy to take on and off. For example, people who use wheelchairs may wear a backless coat so they do not have to stand to take it on and off.

▶ *Some support workers choose to work as a personal assistant. They work with one particular person on a regular basis.*

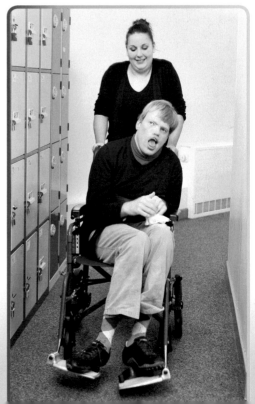

EVERYDAY TASKS

If you are supporting a person in their own home you will be expected to help with a variety of domestic tasks. This might include cooking meals, washing up and housework, such as dusting or hoovering.

Here (above) I am loading the washing machine. Washing, ironing and making beds are all part of the job. I might also help people go shopping for food or clothes. As a support worker, your job is to help people be as independent as possible.

Some people need help to manage their money, and pay bills such as gas, electricity or water. I help people read post, keep track of appointments, write letters and emails, or send cards to their relatives. Although many people I support can't write, some can tell me what they want to say and sign their names.

It is important to allow people to do everything they can for themselves. Sometimes people need encouragement to give them the confidence to do things.

▼ *I help a woman buy herself lunch from the sandwich van. I am always there and ready to help people when they need assistance.*

KEEPING MOBILE

Support workers have to support some people with their **mobility**. The assistance needed varies from person to person.

There are many handling techniques that we have to learn. Some people need simple support getting out of a chair. For others we use special equipment to assist their movement. Some wear a handling belt, which we hold on to, to help them keep their balance as they walk (right). Others can walk independently by holding on to a frame with wheels.

We support people to get out and about. Sometimes I drive them in the car or we use **public transport**. Some people have access to a minibus service.

People who use wheelchairs can be helped on and off the minibus using a tail lift (below).

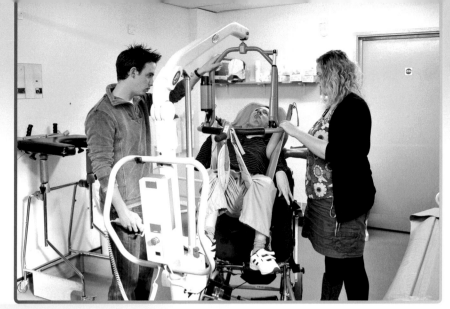

TOOLS OF THE TRADE

We help people with more severe physical disabilities move using a machine called a hoist (above). We attach a sling underneath the person's arms and legs, fasten the straps securely, and clip the sling on to the machine. Then we can press buttons to move the person up and down gently.

New technology helps to keep people independent. A stand aid (left) is a machine that helps people with reduced mobility to stand up. A comfortable sling is fitted round them and as they stand they hold on to the machine, which rises slowly.

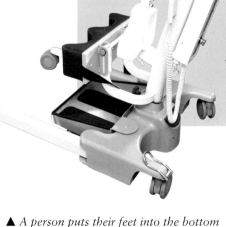

▲ *A person puts their feet into the bottom of the stand aid machine and holds on to the handlebars to raise themselves.*

KEY SKILLS

GOOD FITNESS – You do not have to be very strong physically, but good health and fitness is an advantage as it can be an active job.

ACTIVITIES

Support workers help with a wide range of activities. We support people to make plans about what they want to do with their time. Some people need help with things like getting a job or becoming more independent. Other people want support with leisure and social activities.

At the day centre or in the local community I support people with activities ranging from sports, such as badminton (above), football and darts, to music, creative writing, arts and crafts, gardening and **voluntary** work. We encourage people to try new things and people can change their activities whenever they like.

KEY SKILLS

GOOD ORGANISATION –
To help arrange trips and activities, support workers need to be well organised and have good timekeeping.

▶ *Taking activity sessions such as music or dance is noisy, but great fun.*

Support workers also help people to think about and plan one-off activities, such as trips to the theatre or nights out with friends. We sometimes support people to go on holiday. The walking group recently went to North Wales to walk in the Snowdonia National Park (below).

WORKING CONDITIONS

The hours we work depend on the type of support work we are doing. You may work night shifts, during the evening or at weekends. The number of people you support can vary too. Sometimes you may be with just one person and at other times with a larger group.

▶ *In some places people use an alarm system with a button that they can press to summon help.*

▲ *Sometimes support workers 'sleep-in' at people's houses in case help is needed during the night.*

You need mental and physical **stamina** for the job. Support workers are on their feet all day, moving around. **Emotionally** the work can be hard too. Some people have behaviours that can be a challenge to support.

We have training in how to support someone who is angry or aggressive. This is usually by calming the situation down. A technique I use is to distract a person and help them find something else to turn their attention to.

A support worker often has a high level of independence, especially when working with individuals out in the community. You have to be confident in your ability to deal with difficult

situations and know when to call for help. I always carry a mobile phone.

▼ *In a training session I am taught break away techniques which I might have to use if a situation became aggressive.*

HOW DO I BECOME A SUPPORT WORKER?

You do not have to hold any qualifications to become a support worker. Getting a job depends more on your attitude and having the necessary skills and experience.

I started care work as a volunteer visiting the elderly. Then I volunteered for a children's charity that supported children with learning disabilities. I decided I liked it, and found my first proper job working in a home for the elderly. Next I began working in the day centre.

■ New support workers undergo an **induction** programme. In the first week you **shadow** a colleague to observe and learn. For the next few weeks you are supervised as you work, because learning each individual's needs takes time.

▲ Some people use a frame with wheels to help them get about.

▲ Matt is currently training, so I check that he supports the person correctly.

■ Until you are fully trained there are certain things you cannot do. At the beginning of your training you have to complete courses in moving and handling, hygiene, and health and safety. Over time you complete further courses relevant to your job, such as **first aid** or communication.

■ You can work towards a *Level 2* and *Level 3 Diploma in Health and Social Care*. This will give you a good chance to progress to managerial roles, such as team leader where you manage other support workers.

◄ Here are my first aid and communication certificates.

KEY SKILLS

PASSION FOR CARING –
If you have a genuine desire to help people then this career may be for you.

GLOSSARY

confidential Strictly secret.

coordinate Combine various views and opinions to form a plan.

emotionally Relating to the way you feel.

first aid Help given to a sick or injured person.

hygiene The practice of keeping yourself and your surroundings clean.

independent Acting for oneself and not having to rely on other people for support.

induction A process where someone is introduced to their new job and the roles they will carry out.

learning disabilities A person with learning disabilities has a condition which makes it difficult for them to gain certain skills.

mobility The ability to move.

physical disabilities A person with physical disabilities has trouble using their body to do certain tasks.

public transport Buses, trains and other forms or transport that are available to the public.

risk assessment A consideration of the possible risks in a certain situation.

sensitive Aware of people's feelings.

shadow Follow someone and watch them closely to learn new skills.

social worker A professional who helps people in the community to get the support they need.

speech therapist A professional who helps people who have difficulties with speaking, eating or drinking.

stamina The ability to do physical or mental work for a long period of time.

voluntary Doing a job or helping someone without being paid.

INDEX